Hell Fighters

Also by Michael L. Cooper

Bound for the Promised Land
The Great Black Migration

From Slave to Civil War Hero
The Life and Times of Robert Smalls

Playing America's Game
The Story of Negro League Baseball

MICHAEL L. COOPER

Hell Fighters

African American Soldiers in World War I

Lodestar Books

Dutton   New York

to Wayne and Eric

Library of Congress Cataloging-in-Publication Data

Cooper, Michael L., 1950–
    Hell Fighters: African American soldiers in World War I/Michael L. Cooper
      p. cm.
    1st ed.
    Includes bibliographical references and index.
    Summary: Describes the experiences of African Americans who joined the military during World War I and their fight against both the Germans and racism.
    ISBN 0-525-67534-5 (alk. paper)
    1. World War, 1914–1918—Afro-Americans—Juvenile literature.
2. World War, 1914–1918—Participation, Afro-American—Juvenile literature.   3. Afro-American soldiers—Juvenile literature. [1. World War, 1914–1918—Participation, Afro-American. 2. Afro-American soldiers.]
I. Title.
D639.N4C66   1997
940.4'03—dc 20   96-29082   CIP   AC

Published in the United States by Lodestar Books,
an affiliate of Dutton Children's Books,
a member of Penguin Putnam Inc.,
375 Hudson Street, New York, New York 10014

Published simultaneously in Canada
by McClelland & Stewart, Toronto

Editor: Virginia Buckley   Designer: Dick Granald

Printed in Mexico   First Edition   10 9 8 7 6 5 4 3 2

Contents

North Sea

Amsterdam

Utreck

Doorn

Arnheim

HOLLAND

Tilburg

Zeebrugge

Ostend

Antwerp

Scheldt River

Dusseldorf

Lys River

Ypres

Oudenarde

Lessines

BELGIUM

Brussels

Cologne

Bonn

Aachen

Lille

Mons

Ville-sur-Haine

Namur

Liège

Verviers

Lens

Drocourt

Arras

Douai

Valenciennes

Spa

Meuse River

GERMANY

Rhine River

Quéant

Cambrai

Le Câteau

Péronne

St. Quentin

Amirn

Somme River

F R A N C E

Waldlincourt

Sedan

LUXEMBOURG

Moselle River

Compiègne

Laon

Juvigny

Craonne

Aisne River

CHEMIN DES DAMES

Argonne Forest

Thionville

Soissons

Reims

Verdun

Metz

Oise River

Belleau Wood

Torcy

Marne River

Essey

St. Mihiel

Salient du Feys

Seine River

Paris

0   15   30

STATUTE MILES

Meuse River

Nancy

Meurthe River

Moselle River

W — E

S

——— The front line on August 30, 1918

– – – The armistice line, November 11, 1918

World War I Front Line–1918

African American soldiers marching to battle. Overhead, camouflage has been hung to obscure the men from the enemy's observation airplanes. NATIONAL ARCHIVES

The Great War

World War I was called the Great War. It was, at the time, the biggest and deadliest conflict in history. The war began after the assassination of Archduke Franz Ferdinand in the eastern European city of Sarajevo. His murder in the summer of 1914 ignited long smoldering rivalries between three of the world's most powerful nations—Germany, France, and Great Britain.

The confident German army, expecting quick victory, swept through Belgium and into northern France. Six hundred thousand German soldiers charged into four hundred thousand French, British, and Belgian soldiers. Weeks of fierce fighting left a half million casualties, but neither side could overpower the other. The foes dug in for a four-year standoff, characterized by months of boredom alternating with weeks of horrible fighting.

The war divided the world into two camps. Germany was joined by Turkey and by the Austro-Hungarian Empire. United together they were called the Central Powers. The opposing side was called the Allies. The largest Allied nations were France, Russia, Italy, Japan, and Great Britain. The United States joined the Allies in the third year of the war.

While World War I battles were fought in many countries, most of the fighting occurred on two fronts. Germany invaded the Russian Empire, and for three years the two nations battled each other in a region called the Eastern Front.

The armies of France, Great Britain, and, eventually, the United States were massed on the Western Front, a sliver of southern Belgium and northern France where the invaders had been stopped. Here, the Allies and their enemies, the German and Austrian soldiers, faced each other from two lines of trenches that stretched

1

five hundred miles from the English Channel to the Swiss Alps. The trenches were separated by only a few hundred yards of ground called no-man's-land.

World War I took a terrible toll in human lives. Nine million soldiers and five million civilians died. A whole generation of young European men was killed.

The war toppled old governments and shaped the course of history for much of the twentieth century. The political instability of postwar Germany contributed to the rise to power of the dictator Adolf Hitler. His brutal regime killed millions of Jews, Gypsies, homosexuals, and handicapped people in concentration camps. This atrocity came to be called the Holocaust. And, only twenty-one years after World War I, Hitler's Germany again invaded France, at the beginning of World War II.

People of many races fought in the Great War. They included nearly a million black men from British and French colonies in Africa. Africans were among France's highest ranking army officers.

America, which had been supporting the Allies with vast shipments of food and ammunition, officially entered World War I on April 6, 1917, by declaring war on Germany. At that time, the United States had a very small army—only 130,000 men. By the end of the year, nearly four million men had either volunteered or been drafted into the army.

Some 400,000 of these soldiers were black. They were the largest number of African Americans ever in the military. Nearly 40,000 black soldiers became combat troops. They fought in France in the Ninety-second and Ninety-third Infantry Divisions. But the majority of black soldiers, because of their race, were assigned jobs as laborers at military bases in France and the United States.

The war was doubly difficult for these African Americans. They had to endure danger and hardships while burdened by their own country's racism. Black soldiers were just a small part of the Great War. Yet, while often overlooked, their bravery in battle and their work behind the front lines were significant contributions to their country's role in World War I.

1 A Ragtag Regiment

The Fifteenth New York Voluntary Infantry Regiment was treated like an orphan for most of its short life. "The self-made regiment," said its commander, Colonel William Hayward, "started without traditions, without education, and without friends."

New York's African American National Guard troop was barely a year old in 1917 when the United States officially entered World War I. Few could have predicted that this hastily organized group of men would return from the European conflict as heroes.

The guardsmen learned the fundamentals of army life by meeting nights and weekends at a makeshift armory. It was not spacious like the white National Guard's brick-and-concrete armory downtown. The Harlem armory consisted of an old second-floor dance hall at 132nd Street and Seventh Avenue and, one block away, a former cigar store with a sign in the window that seemed to plead, "RECRUITS WANTED."

The first men to join the Fifteenth were given the rank of sergeant, although they knew as little about army life as the privates under their command. Few of the new guardsmen had proper uniforms. Some of them wore cartridge belts or bayonet scabbards. And when the regiment marched along Harlem's streets, most of the men carried broomsticks instead of rifles.

Harlem residents regarded the Fifteenth New York with a mixture of curiosity and pride. The guardsmen wore civilian clothes and did not march very well, but they were the only African American National Guard regiment in the state and one of just six in the nation.

New York State's governor had created the Fifteenth a couple of years earlier at the urging of black leaders. He appointed a white lawyer, William Hayward, as the regiment's commander. Hayward, a forty-year-old friend of the governor's who had little military experience, was given the rank of colonel.

Colonel Hayward recruited other influential white men. Robert E. Lee's grandson, Dr. George Bolling Lee, was regimental physician. Hayward also persuaded young Hamilton Fish, whose family had been prominent in New York since the colonial era, to join by giving him the rank of captain. Fish's only previous experience leading men had been as the captain of the football team at Harvard University. Another officer was Arthur W. Little, who had been a magazine publisher in civilian life.

These men enlisted in the National Guard because they expected the United States to go to war in Europe. Most citizens did not want to get involved in a conflict that was so far away. Yet the war was going badly for America's traditional friends, France and Great Britain. A million German soldiers were entrenched in France. German submarines had blockaded the British Isles, cutting off shipments of food and other essential goods to the people.

Although officially a "colored" regiment, the Fifteenth was not completely black. The privates and the noncommissioned officers, who were sergeants and corporals, were African American. Some commissioned officers—the lieutenants and captains—were of both races. The majors and the one colonel were all white.

The highest ranking black officer was Captain Napoleon Marshall, a Harvard graduate and a lawyer. Another black officer was Lieutenant Charles W. Fillmore. He was a veteran of the Spanish-American War and one of the businessmen who had urged the governor to create the regiment. A third officer was Lieutenant George B. Lacey. A former Chicago resident, Lacey had been a member of the Eighth Illinois, the nation's largest African American National Guard regiment.

The most famous officer of either color was Lieutenant James Reese Europe. This thirty-nine-year-old musician, known as "Big Jim," was a popular ragtime band leader. After joining the Fifteenth,

Lieutenant Europe recruited fifty musicians to form a regimental band. This band became one of the army's popular attractions.

Colonel Hayward knew a regimental band would help recruitment. He asked friends to donate money to buy instruments. John D. Rockefeller gave $1,000, and a tin can manufacturer gave $10,000. Europe searched the nightclubs of Manhattan, Chicago, and Puerto Rico for talented musicians willing to join the National Guard. One new recruit was the composer Noble Sissle. He was such a good musician he was given the rank of sergeant and soon promoted to lieutenant.

Big Jim's military band always played to large crowds, and, as Colonel Hayward predicted, it attracted recruits. "Hadn't been for that damn band," one soldier later complained, "I wouldn't be in the army."

The biggest aid to recruitment was the declaration of war on April 6, 1917. Thousands of men rushed to join the two military services, the navy and the army. But most were turned away until

Recruits arrive at a Maryland army base. NATIONAL ARCHIVES

African American Soldiers

There were ten thousand black soldiers in the small U.S. army when World War I began. They served in four segregated regiments, which had been created for ex–slaves after the Civil War.

In the 1870s and 1880s, these regiments were stationed at forts in the far West to protect homesteaders and miners from American Indians.

The army sent black regiments to Cuba in 1898 to fight in the summer-long Spanish-American War. Then they sailed them halfway across the Pacific Ocean to the Philippine Islands. There, U.S. soldiers spent four years fighting with Filipinos who were rebelling against American rule.

After the rebels were defeated, the black regiments returned to army forts in Arizona and New Mexico. They remained in the Southwest during the Great War.

The highest ranking black army officer at the beginning of World War I was Colonel Charles Young. He had been the third African American to graduate from the nation's oldest military college, West Point. Young would have been promoted to general if his career had not been sabotaged by prejudice.

As the nation began preparing for war with Germany, Young's superior officers ordered him to take a medical exam. The military doctors concluded the colonel had dangerously high blood pressure, and he had to retire.

Colonel Young vigorously protested the forced retirement. His own doctor insisted the colonel's blood pressure was not unusually high. To prove his fitness, Colonel Young rode a horse from his home in Ohio to Washington, D.C. His protests went unheeded. Many black people believed the colonel had been forced to retire only because the army did not want an African American to become a general.

Colonel Charles Young, at the beginning of World War I, was the army's highest ranking black officer.
NATIONAL ARCHIVES

the military was prepared to train, arm, and house large numbers of new recruits.

Many patriotic black men wanted to join up too, and this worried a lot of white officials. In the past, few blacks had been allowed to join the military. The navy used African American sailors only to cook, wash dishes, or shovel coal in ship boiler rooms. The army had some ten thousand black soldiers serving in four segregated regiments in the remote Southwest. And an African American graduate of West Point, Charles Young, had risen to the rank of colonel. Yet, the thought of arming thousands more black men scared some politicians.

There were long debates over the proper place for blacks in the military. Should they be combat troops or laborers? Should there be black officers? If so, would white men take orders from them? Events did not wait for everyone to agree on answers to these questions.

In the weeks following the declaration of war, hundreds of new recruits joined the Fifteenth New York. Despite the black regiment's

New soldiers are stripped of their civilian clothing and given army clothing.
NATIONAL ARCHIVES

One of the few World War I recruiting posters depicting African Americans

rapid growth, National Guard headquarters often ignored the Fifteenth's requests for supplies. It was particularly upsetting to Colonel Hayward that his men had fewer than two hundred rifles. Then the colonel found a solution to his problem.

The U.S. government, in order to encourage military preparedness, was giving guns to civilian shooting clubs. Hayward forged dozens of letters claiming to represent clubs from all sections of New York City. The federal government sent his fictitious shooting clubs a total of one thousand rifles. The guns arrived just in time for the regiment's first trip to training camp.

Twelve hundred men, on a sunny Sunday in mid-May, marched through the streets of Manhattan to the train station. They were dressed in new olive drab shirts, and their bedrolls were slung from their left shoulders to their right hips. Civilians on their way to church applauded as the guardsmen passed by. At the station, Red Cross workers handed the soldiers cups of coffee, sandwiches, and candy.

The Fifteenth, after a short train ride north to Peekskill, New York, arrived at Camp Whitman at midafternoon. Their first tasks were to pitch tents and dig latrines. Some men had the challenging job of fixing dinner for twelve hundred people with neither cooking supplies nor eating utensils. The colonel's friends in Albany, the state capital, came to the rescue. They arranged delivery of plates, knives, forks, pots, and pans. Dinner was ready by midnight.

Mess call is the customary bugle call in the army to summon soldiers to mess. Mess is army slang for meals. There were no bugle calls at Camp Whitman, one recruit explained, because 90 percent of the men would not have known mess call from reveille, the traditional bugle call to get out of bed in the morning.

Even without a bugler, news that dinner was ready spread quickly. Hungry guardsmen mobbed the mess hall. The officers yelled at the men to quit grabbing food off the tables. The recruits finally formed an orderly line as Colonel Hayward dished out cold canned salmon, beans, and bread.

There was more evidence early the next day that these guardsmen had a lot to learn about military procedure. Many of them were

A young soldier poses proudly.
SCHOMBURG CENTER FOR RESEARCH
IN BLACK CULTURE

waiters, red caps, doormen, and Pullman porters. When they approached a white officer, they would salute and then, in very unmilitary fashion, bow and murmur, "Mawnin' suh, good mawnin'."

The men spent the next two weeks learning to be proper soldiers. They marched on the parade ground and practiced with their rifles at the firing range. By working and living together, they were developing regimental pride. It was a kind of team spirit that would help these soldiers survive on the battlefield. The Fifteenth returned to New York City at the end of May. Soon afterward they were called to active duty in the U.S. Army.

The men were first split up and assigned to guard ammunition depots, shoe factories, and military construction sites in New York and in neighboring New Jersey and Pennsylvania. They were protecting these sites from enemy agents who might try to blow them up to interfere with the nation's war preparations.

The U.S. Army was beginning to recruit, train, and equip a huge new fighting force called the National Army. It would be manned by draftees and by National Guardsmen. These World War I infantrymen were nicknamed doughboys.

Despite the urgent need for soldiers, there was constant discrimination against Colonel Hayward's regiment. He asked that his men be included in the Rainbow Division. This was the first National Army division created by National Guard regiments. It had been dubbed the Rainbow Division because someone remarked that its soldiers came from every state under the rainbow. The Fifteenth could not join, the colonel was told dismissively, because black was not a color of the rainbow.

Hayward also asked to join other New York National Guard regiments in a farewell parade down Manhattan's Fifth Avenue. After being rebuffed again, the colonel made a vow. "Damn their going-away parade! We'll have a parade of our own when we come back—those of us who do come home—and it will be a parade that will make history."

2 Skirmishes in Spartanburg

The men of the Fifteenth groaned when they learned their regiment was being sent for basic training to Camp Wadsworth near Spartanburg, South Carolina. The deep South, where slavery once flourished, was notorious for its cruel treatment of black people. The soldiers knew they would be targets of abuse.

Spartanburg's white citizens, who represented over three quarters of the city's thirty thousand residents, were also apprehensive. The mayor told army officials that the city did not want hundreds of "colored" soldiers, "with their northern ideas about race equality." The mayor feared violence like the recent clash in Houston, Texas. There, one hundred black army men, upset by local police harassment, had marched downtown shooting both policemen and civilians. They killed seventeen white people.

The mayor's protest did not change army orders. In September, the Fifteenth Regiment, along with thirty-five thousand white New York National Guardsmen, boarded ninety-seven special trains for the day-long trip south to Spartanburg. The southern mayor greeted the New Yorkers with a warning: "I can tell you for certain that if any of those colored soldiers go in any of our soda stores and the like and ask to be served, they'll be knocked down. We have our customs down here, and we aren't going to alter them."

Colonel Hayward knew that any incident, no matter who was at fault, would be blamed on his regiment. The colonel gathered his men together at Camp Wadsworth and asked them to raise their right hands and promise to avoid fights regardless of provocation. It proved an impossible promise to keep.

The Houston Riot

"To hell with going to France," one angry soldier shouted to several hundred African American soldiers. "Let's get to work right here."

These men had heard a rumor that two policemen had killed one of their comrades. The local police had been harassing the black soldiers since their arrival a month earlier at Camp Logan, on the outskirts of Houston, Texas.

"Fall in," ordered Sergeant Vida Henry, a thirteen–year army veteran and model soldier. Nearly one hundred men obeyed his order. They loaded their Springfield rifles, attached bayonets, and began the short march into downtown Houston. The infantrymen were searching for the police officers they believed had murdered their comrade.

News spread quickly that armed, angry soldiers were marching through town. It was early evening, and the city's residents were hiding behind locked doors. But at one house, three curious white teenagers, a girl and her two brothers, stood on the front porch peering through the dusk at the passing column of khaki uniforms. The teenagers switched on the porch light to see better. Alarmed by the light, two soldiers wheeled around and fired. A bullet tore through one boy's right arm and another bullet killed his brother. The two boys were the night's first casualties.

Next, the infantrymen surprised four police officers. The soldiers immediately opened fire, wounding two policemen. The other officers fled to the police station. There, an angry crowd of nearly a thousand people had gathered. The mob had looted stores and stolen guns and ammunition. "Let's kill those niggers!" they shouted. "Lynch them from the highest tree!"

Several blocks away, the soldiers met more police officers, including Rufus Daniels, one of the men they believed had killed their comrade earlier that day. Daniels drew his pistol and foolishly charged the infantrymen. A volley of bullets felled the policeman.

A car suddenly rounded the corner. The soldiers raised their rifles as the automobile screeched to a halt, and four men jumped from the car to flee. One was shot down, but three escaped. Another car rounded the corner, and the infantrymen riddled it with bullets, killing an army captain and two white soldiers.

The black troops abruptly lost their enthusiasm. The men knew they would soon face hundreds, maybe thousands of whites, in a terrible fight to the death. Sergeant Henry told his men to return to camp. He then shot and killed himself. The night of violence left seventeen white people and three blacks dead.

The soldiers were arrested and tried for treason in the largest court–martial in American military history. The army court quickly sentenced nineteen black soldiers to hang and sixty–three to life in prison.

Court-martial of black soldiers in Houston
NATIONAL ARCHIVES

People in town constantly harassed the doughboys. One civilian, apparently angered merely by the sight of a black army officer, kicked Captain Marshall off a trolley car. In another incident, a soldier failed to observe the local custom of stepping aside to let whites pass. Two men threw him to the ground and dared him to fight. The black man kept his promise to Colonel Hayward, but white doughboys who saw the incident beat up the two civilians.

It was not unusual for white New Yorkers at Camp Wadsworth to support their Harlem comrades. They even refused to buy cigarettes and soft drinks at stores where black soldiers were not served.

One incident almost led to a deadly confrontation similar to the shootings in Houston. A truck driver working at the army base told soldiers that two members of the Fifteenth had been lynched in front of the police station. Two men were missing and had not been seen since leaving camp the previous day. Some fifty black infantry-men grabbed their rifles and marched into downtown Spartanburg.

Other soldiers rushed to tell Colonel Hayward that his men were attacking the police station. The colonel jumped into a car and sped into town. He found the infantrymen lined up calmly in front of the station. Hayward went inside. One of his soldiers was talking quietly with a police officer. The missing men were not in jail, nor had the police seen them.

The colonel and his troop returned to Camp Wadsworth, where they found the missing soldiers. Walking back from town the previous night, the pair had made a wrong turn and became lost. They had slept in a field.

Just a few days later, there was another serious incident. Lieutenants Jim Europe and Noble Sissle had performed at a downtown church. Afterward, while Europe waited outside, Sissle went into a hotel lobby to buy a newspaper. As he was leaving, the hotel manager rushed toward him screaming, "Say, nigger, don't you know enough to take your hat off." The angry man knocked the lieutenant's cap to the floor and gave the band director a hard kick when he bent over to pick it up.

Sissle tumbled out the hotel door followed by the manager's

curses. This rough treatment of a man in uniform angered white soldiers who were in the lobby. They surrounded the manager, threatening to tear him and his hotel apart.

They were stopped by a loud command, "Attention!" It was Lieutenant Europe. He ordered the soldiers to leave the building. Europe then asked the hotel manager why he had attacked Lieutenant Sissle. Before he would answer, the manager first insisted the band leader remove his hat. Europe hesitated, then slowly took off his cap, explaining that he would comply only to find out what had happened. He had attacked the lieutenant, the red-faced manager angrily replied, because no black man could come into his hotel without removing his hat. Europe, who was over six feet tall and weighed two hundred pounds, looked the shorter man in the eye for several seconds before putting his hat on and slowly walking out the door.

Despite Colonel Hayward's best efforts, and his men's promises, it was apparent there would be a deadly confrontation if black soldiers remained in Spartanburg. The colonel took a train to Washington to explain the volatile situation to army officials. He urged them to send his regiment to France, where troops were badly needed.

On October 24, as trees covering the hills of western South Carolina were turning bright red and orange, the Fifteenth New York marched out of Camp Wadsworth. Thousands of soldiers cheered and serenaded the departing troops with the popular World War I song, "Over There."

> "We're coming over
> and we won't come back
> Till it's over,
> Over There."

It was a touching good-bye salute to comrades going off to battle.

3 Sailing for France

The Fifteenth Regiment's first stop on its way to France was Camp Merritt. This huge New Jersey base had been quickly built that summer to house soldiers from all around the country, while they waited to board troop transports to cross the Atlantic Ocean.

Camp Merritt was larger than many American towns. The rows of two-story wooden barracks lining its streets housed forty thousand soldiers. Nearly one-fourth of all the soldiers shipped overseas, some five hundred thousand men, passed through the camp. Many spent less than a day there before embarking on the voyage to France.

Two weeks after arriving at Camp Merritt, the Fifteenth boarded ferry boats that carried the men down the Hudson River to the Hoboken piers in New York Harbor. During the Great War, Hoboken, New Jersey, was America's busiest port. On one hectic day, fifty-one thousand men were loaded onto seventeen transports. It was, an army man boasted, the most people ever boarded onto ships in a single day in the history of the world.

The Fifteenth's two thousand men stood in line after line. They were looked at by doctors checking for diseases, by intelligence officers checking for spies, and by sergeants checking each soldier's equipment. Their favorite line was at the Red Cross table, where women had been working all night preparing sandwiches, rolls, and coffee for the departing troops. In order to serve so many soldiers, the Red Cross had built the world's biggest coffeemaker; it could brew twenty thousand pounds of ground coffee a day.

The black regiment boarded its ship that afternoon. The dough-boys were sailing on a confiscated German ocean liner, originally named the *Princess Irene*. The liner had been renamed after a Native American princess, *Pocahontas*.

Soldiers of the 371st Infantry waiting in Hoboken, New Jersey, to board a troop ship

Red Cross women distribute food to soldiers waiting to go overseas.
NATIONAL ARCHIVES

Not long after the last soldier had walked up the gangplank, a loud voice over the public address system commanded, "Abandon ship! Abandon ship!" The men grabbed life jackets and ran to the lifeboats. Thousands of soldiers dashed about, bumping into one another and jamming narrow passageways and stairs. After many minutes of confusion, there was an announcement saying the order had been a practice drill. It would be repeated once, twice, even three times each day of the voyage, and the men would never know whether the alarm was a drill or an actual attack.

The biggest threats at sea were German U-boats, or undersea boats, which was the popular name for the first submarines. They prowled beneath the waters along the coast of France and Britain. Their torpedoes sank troop transports, supply ships, and passenger liners suspected of sneaking war supplies to England or France.

One of the worst attacks occurred on May 7, 1915, when a U-boat sank a British passenger ship, the *Lusitania,* killing 1,198 people. The

Germans torpedoed the liner because their spies had learned it was carrying a secret cargo of munitions.

After several delays caused by fire and mechanical problems, the *Pocahontas* finally sailed on December 13, 1917, a dark day of snow and freezing, gale-force winds. As the transport got under way, the soldiers stayed below deck so any German spies watching the harbor would not spot the troopship and relay the information to U-boat captains.

The *Pocahontas* joined a convoy of seven vessels, which carried supplies and more soldiers. Some thirty-five thousand American troops crossed the Atlantic in convoys that December. All the ships were painted with bold geometric patterns, called dazzle camouflage, designed to create optical illusions that would make ships harder to hit with torpedoes.

The men aboard the *Pocahontas* slept in bunk beds stacked three, four, and five high. Extra beds had been added to every possible space in the hallways and even in the galley. The following summer, when there was an increase in the number of troops being

One doughboy completing last-minute paperwork, or perhaps writing a quick letter home
NATIONAL ARCHIVES

A German U-boat prowls in the Atlantic Ocean. NATIONAL ARCHIVES

Church service for stevedores, who are wearing life jackets, on the top deck of a troop transport NATIONAL ARCHIVES

shipped overseas, the transports were so full the doughboys had to share bunks. A man slept in a bed for twelve hours, then another soldier took his turn, sleeping in the same bed for the next twelve hours.

The men had little to do during the crossing. It was too cold to stay on deck. Down below was dark and crowded. The smell of sweat and cigarette smoke filled the air. No lights were permitted at night. The monotony of the voyage was broken only by lifeboat drills and meals, which were served twice a day, at midmorning and at mid-afternoon.

After two weeks at sea, on Sunday, December 23rd, the convoy entered the danger zone. U-boats lurked in this area near the English coast. At church services that morning, the men stood on deck in the cold wind and sang familiar hymns: "Onward Christian Soldiers," "Nearer My God to Thee," and "Rock of Ages."

The men awoke December 25th to a very welcome sight. Seven Allied destroyers, bristling with big guns, had joined the convoy on the last leg of its trip. Overhead, English airplanes and dirigibles searched for U-boats lurking beneath the shallow coastal waters.

Two days later, the ship steamed into the safe harbor at Brest, France. The men crowded onto the deck. Few of them had ever visited a foreign country. They were eager to see the old port and the big stone châteaus, or mansions, overlooking the harbor. The picturesque town made the men forget for a moment that they had come to this country to fight a war.

④ Over There

On New Year's Day, Jim Europe's band played "Auld Lang Syne" and the ship's crew waved good-bye as the Harlem regiment filed down the gangplank into Brest. The long line of doughboys marched briskly through the old city's narrow streets.

Along the way, they saw a few children and elderly people. The women they passed were dressed in somber black, in mourning for the million countrymen who had been killed in forty months of war. All able-bodied men were away serving in the French army. Some citizens welcomed the doughboys by shouting, *"Vive les Américains."* Others were bitter; more soldiers, they said, only meant more fighting.

At the train station, the New Yorkers climbed aboard a long train of small boxcars. Some asked about the meaning of the words "Cheveaux 8 Hommes 40," printed on the side of each car. They literally meant, one soldier who understood the French language explained, "eight horses forty men." The doughboys jokingly wondered where the eight horses would fit since only thirty men, and their heavy backpacks, had managed to squeeze into each boxcar.

The French trains were not only small, they were also slow. The men rode for seventeen hours in the cold, cramped, and dark cars. They arrived in the coastal city of Saint-Nazaire at three the following morning.

The soldiers stretched their legs marching two miles through the silent, snow-covered town to Camp Cöetquidan. They were greeted at the camp by dozens of black Americans who filled their tin cups with steamy hot coffee. These men were cooks, up early preparing the camp's breakfast. They were some of the several thousand African Americans in Saint-Nazaire.

A French train takes American soldiers to training camp. NATIONAL ARCHIVES

Black stevedores had been among the first Americans rushed to France. More black laborers arrived every month. By summer 1918, there would be fifty thousand African Americans in Saint-Nazaire alone. They worked alongside tens of thousands of Chinese, Spaniards, French peasant women, and German prisoners.

All of these people were needed to supply the French, British, and United States armies in France. They also were preparing for the arrival of three million American soldiers. This new force would require huge amounts of clothing, food, and ammunition. The war could be won or lost on the Allies' ability to supply their armies.

The work was never ending. Stevedores unloaded the transports that were crowded into the harbor. Other laborers constructed a mile-long pier so more ships could be unloaded faster. The cargo was

Laborers in Uniform

There was a clear military policy, one historian has observed, to make black soldiers "laborers in uniform." The army decided in late 1917 that most black draftees would not be combat troops. It assigned three out of every four African Americans to stevedore and labor companies.

The men in these companies were made the butt of jokes by combat troops. Yet, delivering food, clothing, and other supplies to the American Expeditionary Force was a vital job.

Stevedore and labor battalions were rushed to France to prepare the way for American infantrymen. They quickly enlarged French ports, built new railroads, and constructed huge warehouses. One typical storage depot covered six square miles and required twenty-five thousand men to operate.

Thousands of black soldiers worked alongside tens of thousands of French women, German prisoners of war, Chinese men, and other nationalities unloading the many ships that arrived daily. In the busy summer of 1918, when two hundred fifty thousand soldiers a month were arriving in France, shifts of stevedores toiled around the clock.

American generals planned to send at least four million doughboys overseas. The army would need mountains of supplies from America. In just twelve months, it was estimated the AEF would consume 500 million pounds of beef, 570 million pounds of potatoes, and 30,528,000 gallons of coffee. The AEF's half million horses had to eat too; they would need four billion pounds of hay.

These laborers in uniform had been the first Americans to arrive in France and the last to leave. They performed difficult and essential work but never received the recognition they deserved.

Doughboys peeling potatoes in France
NATIONAL ARCHIVES

Stevedores unloading bales of hay at a French port
NATIONAL ARCHIVES

A soldier works as a blacksmith shoeing a horse.
NATIONAL ARCHIVES

stored in newly constructed warehouses. In machine shops, men were rapidly assembling American-made locomotives and boxcars. These trains would travel on new railroad tracks, rushing food, ammunition, and medical supplies to the battlefront in northern France.

The Fifteenth was put to work building a dam and reservoir. There was a shortage of laborers, and the men feared they, like other black soldiers, would be assigned permanently to pick-and-shovel work.

James Europe and his band were the first to escape labor duty. They were sent to Aix-les-Bains, a rest camp for Allied troops. The concerts, both for soldiers and for French citizens, proved so popular that the band was sent on tour. Over the next six months, the musicians visited twenty-five cities, performing in hospitals, military camps, and concert halls.

Rest and recreation were important for all soldiers. Most camps had YMCAs. The larger Ys provided libraries where men gathered to read, write letters, and play games. A snack bar served hot chocolate, lemonade, and cake. These Ys were staffed by some of the twenty-

Lieutenant James Reese Europe and his band perform for French citizens in a town square.
NATIONAL ARCHIVES

five thousand American women who volunteered to go to France and work without pay to help the American Expeditionary Force, or AEF.

Many Ys did not welcome black soldiers. Some restricted their hours, while others posted signs stating "No Negroes Allowed." The only all-black YMCA in France was at Saint-Nazaire, and it was managed by the Reverend D. Leroy Ferguson of Louisville, Kentucky. It was appropriate that a preacher supervised the facility because part of the YMCA's mission was to protect doughboys from drinking and prostitutes.

Camp commanders also tried to protect their soldiers from vice by restricting visits to neighboring towns and cities, where the French government operated brothels for its soldiers.

Some commanders prohibited black doughboys from leaving camp while off duty. But they could not keep French citizens from befriending African Americans, so one officer distributed a letter among village mayors. In it he explained that in the United States whites, especially women, did not socialize with blacks, and he asked the French to honor this custom. This attempt to segregate the soldiers from French citizens did not work. It merely added to the resentment black doughboys felt for their white officers.

The men of the Fifteenth were anxious to leave Saint-Nazaire. They complained daily that they should be carrying rifles not shovels. Colonel Hayward tried to bolster the regiment's morale. He organized baseball games, boxing matches, and tug-of-war contests. The colonel also ordered weekly dress parades and awarded prizes for the neatest uniforms. But Hayward, like his men, also wanted to be at the front.

The colonel wrote a long letter to General John "Black Jack" Pershing. The general was in charge of the American Expeditionary Force. Hayward thought Pershing might be especially sympathetic to African American soldiers. The general had been given his nickname, Black Jack, during the 1898 Spanish-American War because he had commanded black soldiers in Cuba.

The colonel's letter, in addition to saying his troops were ready

A game of tug-of-war relieves the boredom of camp life. NATIONAL ARCHIVES

and eager to fight, included an unusual bit of information. Knowing the general was a fanatic about preventing venereal disease, Hayward explained his men had not reported a new case of syphilis or gonorrhea in over three months.

General Pershing, responding more to the demands of French generals than to Hayward's letter, assigned the black regiment to the French army, which badly needed fresh troops.

The only U.S. soldiers to serve under French command were the Fifteenth New York and the three other black regiments of the Ninety-third Division. Other American infantrymen were being held in reserve until there was a large enough force—about one million men—for General Pershing to command his own army on the battlefield. Pershing's AEF did not go into battle until August of 1918. Some Americans, though, were rushed to the front to help the British and French during the big German offenses that spring and summer.

In the winter of 1917–1918, Germany had moved a half million soldiers from Russia to France. Its three-year war against Russia had ended when the Bolshevik Revolution overthrew the czar, Russia's traditional ruler. A new government was established that made peace with the German government.

The transferred soldiers reinforced nearly a million German troops massed on the Western Front. German generals knew they might lose the war if they failed to conquer France before many fresh U.S. fighting men were sent to battle.

It was a very grave time. People feared the exhausted French and British armies would collapse under a German attack. "When we first landed in France," an officer in the Fifteenth New York, Major Arthur W. Little, noted in his diary, "she was so sick of body and at heart that the common people of the towns and the soldiers of the ranks not only sensed defeat but admitted it."

5 On the Western Front

The Fifteenth Regiment left Saint-Nazaire in early March. It traveled once again in the small boxcars marked "CHEVEAUX 8 HOMMES 40" four hundred miles north to training camp near the battlefront, at Chalons. The Harlem regiment was warmly welcomed.

"Our great American general put the black orphan in a basket, set it on the doorstep of the French, pulled the bell, and went away," one of the Fifteenth's officers told a French colonel wearing an "ENGLISH SPOKEN HERE" sign. And the colonel replied, "Welcome little black baby."

The French did not discriminate against black people as white Americans did. Over a half million blacks from France's African colonies had joined the French army. These colonials served at all ranks, including four colonels and two generals.

The New Yorkers had to adjust to new equipment and different customs. They thought French rifles were inferior to U.S. Army rifles. The Americans also complained about the Gallic habit of eating only soup and bread for dinner. But the men did enjoy one French custom—wine with meals.

The French customarily drink wine at lunch and dinner, so each day their soldiers received a canteen full of red wine. Instead of dividing it between the two meals, as the Frenchmen did, the Americans often drank theirs all at once. One doughboy alarmed the whole camp when, after gulping the contents of his canteen, he began shooting at imaginary Germans. French commanders decided against giving the Americans wine; instead, they would receive a daily ration of sugar to use in their coffee.

The New Yorkers spent five weeks training. French instructors,

32

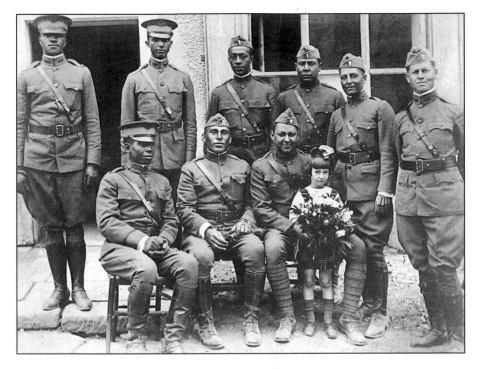

Army officers posing with a French child NATIONAL ARCHIVES

Doughboys learn to use gas masks. Poison gas was a common weapon in World War I. NATIONAL ARCHIVES

Bayonet practice prepares men for hand-to-hand combat.
NATIONAL ARCHIVES

assisted by translators, taught them about trench warfare, poison gas, and hand-to-hand combat. As they had been at Saint-Nazaire, the men were impatient to get to the fighting.

They constantly heard field cannons, which made deep rumbling noises like the sound of distant thunder, booming in the distance. A huge German attack was under way. "The boys keep looking at the big flashes in the north, and saying 'goddamn, le's go,'" Major Little noted in his diary, "and we've formally adopted 'le's go' as the motto of this brunette fighting outfit."

AEF commanders gave the Fifteenth a new name, the 369th Regiment, U.S. Army, and in mid-April ordered it to the front. There the 369th would serve under General Henri Gouraud. The general had lost his right arm early in the war. He was a national hero. French soldiers, who called Gouraud the Lion of France, cheered whenever they saw him.

While marching to their positions at the front, the 369th came under fire for the first time. Artillery shells from German cannons eight to ten miles away whistled through the air and exploded nearby. The men's reaction surprised Major Little. They were "never really scared," he said, but "laughed and screamed in gleeful excitement."

As the Americans neared the front lines, they saw the awful devastation of war. Artillery barrages had reduced villages, which had been standing for hundreds of years, to rubble. The surrounding fields in previous springs would have been freshly plowed and sown with wheat. The countryside, one soldier said, had been "torn and horribly disfigured by shell burst or by pick and shovel." Instead of crops, there were thousands of little wooden crosses, each one marking a soldier's grave.

The 369th joined French soldiers at a camp only a few miles from the German army. The camp consisted of trenches and dugouts, which were underground shelters where the men slept. Some dugouts were furnished with beds, rugs, tables, chairs, and oil lamps looted from deserted homes. The trenches and the dugouts protected infantrymen from the flying shrapnel of exploding shells continuously fired by distant enemy artillery.

The French soldiers were glad to see the Americans. They had been fighting for three and one-half years. Many were dispirited. Some

Men of the 369th outside a dugout several miles behind the front line
NATIONAL ARCHIVES

had committed mutiny the previous winter by refusing to go to the front. The Allies were worried that the French army would rebel against its generals. The doughboys' arrival gave the French new confidence and stopped the threat of rebellion.

Soldiers stationed near the front took turns at guard duty in the trenches on the edge of a narrow stretch of earth called no-man's-land. Where there had been a lot of fighting, no-man's-land was a forlorn area of mud, shell craters, splintered trees, and barbed wire. On the opposite side, only a few hundred feet away, German soldiers guarded their own trench row.

The Allies and Central Powers had been in a stalemate. The two enemies occupied similar lines of trenches nearly five hundred miles long. Each side had tried to overwhelm the other by sending hundreds of thousands of men into battle. But the armies were almost equally matched, and only a few miles of ground were ever won or lost.

The killing, on the other hand, was horrendous. Artillery and machine guns were used to slaughter huge numbers of men. The battle of the Somme, one of the war's worst battles, began in July of 1916. It lasted six months, and casualties on both sides exceeded one million men.

These big battles, though, were infrequent. Most of the time soldiers manned muddy or dusty trenches and waited for something to happen. Day-to-day life was miserable. The men complained the most about rain and rats. It rained so often soldiers developed trench foot, a numbing of the feet caused by standing for long periods in mud and water.

Thousands of rats boldly scurried about. They ate everything, from decomposing corpses to boots. Rats even gnawed through sleeping men's pants pockets searching for food.

The men also complained about cooties, or body lice, which infested every frontline soldier. On warm spring days, bare-chested men passed the time by "reading the shirt." They would hold their shirts up to the light as though reading a newspaper, but they were looking for lice.

Boredom became so unbearable that men sometimes took foolish chances for a little entertainment. One night, French soldiers heard a band playing on the German side. They crawled across no-man's-land and stopped beneath the barbed wire strung in front of the enemy's trenches to listen to the concert. The excursion ended when the Germans discovered their uninvited guests and tossed grenades over the wire.

Enemy fire and accidents killed or wounded someone every few days. Once, a soldier knocked a bag of grenades into a dugout where several members of the 369th were sleeping, and the explosion injured three men.

Raiding parties were another constant danger. Under the cover of darkness, enemy troops would sneak across to kill or capture Allied soldiers. The 369th had been on the front line for nearly a month when two of its men became heroes for repelling German raiders.

On the night of May 13, Privates Henry Johnson and Needham Roberts were on guard duty while three other men slept in a nearby dugout. Roberts heard the sound of wire cutters clipping barbed wire just a few yards away. As he yelled a warning to his sleeping comrades, a flare exploded overhead, signaling the raiders to attack.

The light from the flare revealed Germans, armed with pistols and knives, rushing through a gap in the barbed wire. The enemy soldiers lobbed grenades into the trenches, wounding both Americans. One explosion collapsed the front of the dugout, trapping the three men inside.

Roberts, though badly wounded, propped himself against the dugout door and threw a grenade at the approaching raiders. Johnson quickly fired all three shots from his rifle. Just after the last shot, a German soldier lunged at him. The American used his rifle as a club and splintered the wooden stock across his attacker's head.

Johnson saw two enemy soldiers picking up Roberts to carry him away as a prisoner. He leaped on one German's back and plunged his nine-inch bolo knife into the top of the man's head.

By then, the man Johnson had knocked down with his rifle was on his feet, shooting at the American. A bullet hit the doughboy's

Remains of a German soldier hanging on barbed wire
LIBRARY OF CONGRESS

side, and he sank to his knees. The attacker rushed over to finish off the fallen man. As the grim-faced German hesitated over the dough-boy, Johnson summoned all of his strength and lunged upward, thrusting his already bloody knife into the man's gut. The other raiders, hearing the sound of approaching soldiers, fled back across no-man's-land.

The French government awarded both Johnson and Roberts the Croix de Guerre, a medal bestowed for heroism and gallantry. Reporters interviewed the two men in their hospital beds. Stories about the fight appeared in many U.S. newspapers and magazines. Because the war's horrible battles were frequently described as hells, and the enemy described as devils, African American newspapers began calling the 369th Hell Fighters. It was a nickname the Harlem regiment proudly accepted. "Our colored volunteers from Harlem," Major Little observed, "had become in a day one of the famous fight-ing regiments of the World War." Henry Johnson and Needham Roberts were the first men in the 369th Regiment to win medals for bravery, but not the last.

6 Summer 1918

On July 14, French soldiers uncorked bottles of champagne to share with the 369th. They were celebrating Bastille Day, a French holiday similar to America's Fourth of July. The celebration was a brief distraction from the war, which had become very fierce in the previous four months.

In March, German troops had smashed through the British defenses near Belgium. They fought their way to within thirty-two miles of Paris. Their artillery was shelling the capital for the first time during the war. Retreating Frenchmen cried, *"la guerre est finie,"* the war is over. But French and British forces, supported by several thousand American marines and army infantrymen, had fought determinedly to stop the Germans from capturing Paris, the nation's most important city.

Bastille Day proved to be the war's turning point. Captured German soldiers had revealed that their army, hoping to catch the Allies off guard during the holiday celebration, was preparing a major surprise attack at midnight. The French planned a surprise of their own.

They knew German cannons would bombard the frontline trenches that night to kill as many men as possible before their infantry attacked at daybreak. After dark, Allied soldiers quietly withdrew from the front line to avoid the barrage. A few Frenchmen remained behind so the Germans would not suspect the trenches were empty. These men faced almost certain death.

At 11:55 P.M., the Allies unleashed their own artillery barrage. At midnight, German cannons started shelling the Allies. The battle of

One of the many French villages destroyed by artillery fire NATIONAL ARCHIVES

the Champagne region had begun. Along a fifty-mile front the big guns on both sides roared for seven hours.

At daybreak, thousands of German infantry swarmed through the shroud of smoke that hung over no-man's-land. The attackers easily overran the first line of trenches, killing or capturing the few Allied soldiers they found.

The confident Germans charged ahead, straight into a second line of troops. The two armies lashed out at each other. "Never have I seen so many dead men, never such frightful scenes," a German officer said. The exhausted and disorganized enemy withdrew after three days.

The Allies immediately attacked their retreating foe. They killed an estimated thirty thousand of the enemy on the first day of the counterattack. The French army pushed the Germans back five miles, capturing four hundred cannons and nineteen thousand soldiers.

The mid-July German attack and the French counterattack plunged the 369th into the horrors of battle. The men of the Harlem regiment crouched in shallow trenches during the artillery barrage. In his diary Major Little wrote that "hell was at work" that night. The black soldiers were helpless. There was no escape from the shells exploding constantly around them. They hugged the earth, expecting at any moment to die.

An exploding phosphorous bomb lights up the night. NATIONAL ARCHIVES

The soldiers were even more terrified later, during the poison gas attack. The Germans released nine thousand tons of poisonous gases during the battle. Some gases killed or blinded their victims. Other kinds, such as mustard gas, burned skin, lungs, and eyes so badly that men were disabled for weeks.

At the first warning of a gas attack, the soldiers of the 369th quickly put on their masks. Many were convinced they would be killed by the gas seeping in all around them. Some cried in anticipation of the pain, while others stretched out quietly on the ground waiting to die. But the gas proved harmless and soon drifted away.

While no one from the 369th died in the gas attack, many men from the Harlem regiment died in the artillery barrage and in the Allied counterattack. Death had become so common that the living paid little attention. After "four months of frontline defensive work," Major Little admitted, "my heart had become hardened to the loss of human life in general."

The July battle was the last major German attack of the war. The Kaiser's army suffered 800,000 casualties in the spring and summer offenses. The Central Powers were running out of soldiers. Boys as young as fourteen and fifteen were being sent into battle.

The British and French armies on the Western Front had lost 350,000 men during the first half of 1918. But these casualties were being replaced that summer by a quarter of a million American soldiers arriving in France each month. The Allies knew the German army was weak, so they planned one big knockout blow.

7 The Last Battle

Before daybreak on September 26, the American, British, and French armies began the biggest attack of the war—the battle of the Meuse-Argonne. Four thousand cannons had been pounding the Germans since midnight. In the following seven weeks, the Allies would fire more artillery shells than the entire Union army used during the Civil War.

Rolling kitchens served the 369th Regiment a quick breakfast of coffee and slum gullion, army slang for a stew of beef, beans, and potatoes. Then the men waited nervously for the infantry attack to begin. They thought about their families back in New York and wondered if they would live to see them again.

At 5:30 A.M., over one million Allied soldiers all along the Western Front began advancing against the Kaiser's army. Trucks, wagons, and men clogged narrow roads. Artillery crews cursed and beat the mules and horses that struggled to pull heavy cannons through mud and shell craters.

Waves of soldiers, gripping their rifles, swept across no-man's-land. The acrid smoke of gunpowder mixed with the morning's heavy fog. Dead men and horses, killed by artillery, littered the ground. The stench of their decaying corpses filled the air.

Gunfire seemed to come from all directions. There was the *pop, pop, pop* of rifles and the *rat-a-tat-tat* of machine guns. Artillery shells fell more rapidly. One type of shell had been dubbed the "Jack Johnson," after the famous African American heavyweight boxer. Jack Johnsons made loud rushing noises, like approaching locomotives, just before slamming into the earth with deafening explosions and spraying steel shrapnel that tore the life from men's bodies.

This man was one of the few black soldiers trained to operate a machine gun. NATIONAL ARCHIVES

The Allies met surprisingly little resistance from their enemy. The first day of the attack some thirty-three thousand Germans surrendered. But in the Argonne Forest, where the Harlem regiment fought, the Kaiser's men battled fiercely against the Americans and French. "Every goddamn German there who didn't have a machine gun had a cannon," one doughboy complained.

The 369th's three battalions were given different assignments. The Second Battalion attacked a ridge called Bellevue Signal. That battle, Captain Hamilton Fish recalled, "raged incessantly for the next forty-eight hours in a horrifying exchange of machine gun and artillery fire."

The First Battalion, under the command of Major Little, hunkered down in a shallow trench while waiting for orders to advance. A steady rain fell on the first day of battle. The soldiers' only shelter

Men of the 369th, wearing distinctive French helmets, prepare for an enemy attack. NATIONAL ARCHIVES

was strips of canvas stretched across the tops of their narrow trench. Food was in short supply. They carried small portions of beef jerky, hardtack, and bouillon cubes. Their canteens were filled with water from a nearby river.

The weather the following morning was clear and cool. As the Harlem doughboys were eating the last of their rations, a runner brought Major Little an order to drive the Germans from the nearby village of Sechault.

The First Battalion advanced in a long single column on the cluster of old stone houses. They were spotted by a German artillery crew. Suddenly, shells were exploding among the Americans, wounding and killing dozens of men.

They pushed ahead through the deadly artillery shower. As they neared Sechault, the men fanned out over a half mile. Major Little

Two Black Combat Divisions

Two divisions of African American combat troops served in France. One division fought under American command and returned to the United States feeling disgraced. The second division fought under French command, and its men returned home feeling like heroes.

The four regiments of the Ninety–second Division were draftees from the South. The division's white commanders thought black draftees, especially Southerners, would never make good soldiers. This attitude contributed to the poor training and low morale of the twenty-six thousand men in the Buffalo division.

At the beginning of the battle of the Meuse–Argonne, three regiments of the Ninety–second were held in reserve while the fourth, the 368th, was sent into combat. The officers in command of the advancing soldiers had strict orders to maintain communications with nearby allies. Early in the battle, the 368th became disorganized and lost contact with the other regiments. Hundreds of its men retreated. The 368th was soon withdrawn from the front line.

The Eighth Illinois Infantry, Chicago's all-black National Guard regiment LIBRARY OF CONGRESS

What had gone wrong? The soldiers argued that they had become lost because they were never given good maps or clear orders. But many people believed the incident proved black men were neither brave enough nor smart enough to be combat soldiers.

Several black officers were charged with desertion. At the court-martial, or military trial, five of them were found guilty and sentenced to death. A later investigation modified the sentence, but the feeling of shame never went away. The whole division was blamed for the 368th's failure. Thirty years afterward, when the military was being desegregated, some people still argued that the 368th's mistakes during the battle of the Meuse-Argonne had proven black men were not good soldiers.

92 DIVISION

The 369th, the 370th, and the 372nd Regiments in the Ninety-third Infantry Divison consisted of African American National Guardsmen from six states, while the fourth, the 371st, was made up of draftees. All four regiments distinguished themselves while assigned to the French army.

93 DIVISION

The 370th, in one battle, captured nineteen hundred German prisoners in a single day. And both the 369th and the 372nd were awarded the Croix de Guerre for their effective fighting during the Meuse–Argonne offensive.

The 371st proved wrong the popular notion that black draftees could not become good soldiers. The regiment was assigned to France's famous Red Hand division. These Frenchmen were given their nickname early in the war after a victorious but bloody hand–to–hand battle. The 371st was worthy of the Red Hand's fierce reputation. Its men were awarded more French medals for bravery than any other American regiment.

The French army bestowed medals for individual bravery on more than five hundred black soldiers in the Ninety–third Division. But these honors were costly. Nearly one third of the division's ten thousand men were killed or wounded.

German soldiers advancing against the Allies NATIONAL ARCHIVES

lay on his back in a muddy trench scribbling orders and handing them to runners, who scurried through the gunfire delivering these messages to company sergeants. A German biplane flew so low overhead the major saw the pilot's face looking down at him. The plane dropped a single bomb that killed and wounded a dozen men.

The soldiers cautiously climbed out of the trench and crept toward the village. They inched along the ground on their stomachs or crawled on their hands and knees, keeping low to avoid the sweep of machine-gun fire.

The men slid into trenches the Germans had dug along the edge of Sechault. They were surprised to find the bloody bodies of twelve men from their Second Battalion. This battalion had briefly laid siege to the village before receiving orders to help French soldiers capture nearby Bellevue Signal ridge.

As the Americans approached one side of Sechault, the Germans

American soldiers, trying to avoid enemy bullets, sprint for cover past a disabled tank and the body of a German soldier. NATIONAL ARCHIVES

withdrew from the opposite side. They then took up new positions in a forest just beyond the village. The woods, fortified by machine-gun nests and trenches, were easier to defend. The enemy kept its guns aimed at the village. Any doughboy who tried to cross a street was greeted by a burst of machine-gun fire.

A runner brought Major Little a message that the French soldiers who were supposed to be protecting his battalion's flanks had fallen behind. His men were so far ahead of all the others, the major realized with alarm, they might be surrounded by the enemy and slaughtered.

That prospect frightened one lieutenant, who confronted Major Little and argued that staying overnight in the village would be suicide. The major replied that he could not withdraw without orders. Afterward, Little overheard a soldier asking his sergeant, "Do you think we're going back?" The sergeant replied, "Hell no, we just got here."

Major Little realized their situation was grim. His men, now completely out of rations, had not eaten since morning. Many of them

German machine-gun crew waiting to surprise Allied soldiers
NATIONAL ARCHIVES

*After a heavy
artillery barrage,
French soldiers
cautiously
inspect German
trenches.*
LIBRARY OF CONGRESS

*American
doughboys
fighting their
way through
the ruins of a
forest*
NATIONAL ARCHIVES

Hundreds of German prisoners heading for an Allied prison camp
NATIONAL ARCHIVES

had been killed or wounded, and they were in danger of being trapped by the enemy.

It was a long, tense night. The enemy fired flares over the village and shot randomly at the Americans. The Germans wanted to keep the doughboys awake, tense, and scared. Several times during the night, the men thought they were being attacked.

At three that morning, the guards heard footsteps. They yelled to the strangers to stop and identify themselves. In heavily accented

*A doughboy
guards German
prisoners.*
NATIONAL ARCHIVES

English a man responded, "Comrades, comrades." The nervous guards, thinking they had caught an enemy raiding party, opened fire. Then they heard several men pleading for them not to shoot. It was a French patrol. The shots had killed one soldier and wounded three others.

Near daybreak, the Americans heard German officers in the forest yelling orders at their men. Word spread through the battalion that the enemy was preparing to attack. "All out for Custer's last stand," one doughboy prodded his comrades with gallows humor.

The men fixed bayonets to their rifles. At any moment they expected to see a mass of gray German uniforms swarming toward them. Instead, enemy artillery began shelling the town, forcing the First Battalion to withdraw from the village.

Major Little sent Colonel Hayward a note requesting that his hungry and exhausted men be relieved. He received a quick reply. Allied artillery would bombard the forest, Hayward ordered, and afterward Little's battalion must advance and clear the enemy from the woods.

The field guns fired only a few shots and then stopped. Although he was surprised there was not more shelling, Major Little prepared to attack. A breathless runner suddenly arrived with new orders. The First Battalion should hold its position until replaced by fresh troops. It was relieved that night by the 363rd Infantry of France. The next morning, after a heavy shelling of the woods, the French soldiers attacked.

The Americans were wet, muddy, cold, and exhausted. They were glad to see a rolling kitchen, even if it was serving only coffee and slum gullion. After breakfast, the battalion began the grim task of gathering its dead.

In three days of battle, in the entire 369th Regiment, a total of 172 men had been killed and 679 wounded. Among the casualties were Lieutenant Charles S. Dean and three of his men; their lifeless bodies were found draped over barbed wire. Dean had been moving his machine-gun company to a safer position. The four men were clipping through the wire when German bullets cut them down.

The survivors traded stories about how their comrades had died and, more encouragingly, how some were heroes. One hero was Captain Fish. He had repeatedly risked his life rescuing the wounded and delivering food to troops under fire. He was awarded America's Silver Star for bravery.

In the attack on Sechault, Lieutenant George S. Robb was wounded three times, yet he insisted on staying with his men. He was given a Congressional Medal of Honor, Robb was one of only seventy-eight men awarded the medal during World War I.

On October 4, Austria and Germany asked for peace. It took five weeks and more fighting before the Central Powers and the Allies could agree on the terms of their peace agreement. Then, at 11 A.M. on November 11 (the eleventh hour of the eleventh day of the eleventh month), 1918, they signed the armistice.

Huge celebrations broke out in Paris, London, and New York. Strangers embraced strangers. Crowds of men and women, waving flags and cheering loudly, paraded endlessly through the streets. The celebration, like a huge New Year's Eve party, lasted all day and all night.

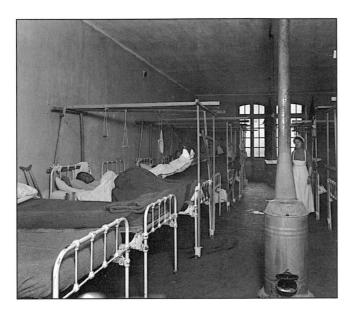

*A wounded soldier
in an army hospital*
NATIONAL ARCHIVES

*French citizens
celebrating the
armistice,
November 11, 1918*
NATIONAL ARCHIVES

As word of peace spread across the battlefields, there was a silent pause, a moment of disbelief. Then soldiers of all nationalities cheered and hugged their comrades. They were alive, and the worst war in the history of mankind was over.

8 Home to Harlem

After the Great War ended, American soldiers stayed in Europe several months longer. While occupying part of Germany and cleaning up the destruction in France, black doughboys were honored by the French and abused by their own countrymen.

The 369th advanced across the snow-covered Vosges Mountains into Germany. The men marched into enemy territory wondering what kind of reception they would receive. They passed through deserted village after deserted village until finally reaching one that was inhabited. Its residents clearly welcomed peace. They had hoisted American flags and displayed photographs of President Woodrow Wilson in their windows. Girls and women, now wearing festive costumes instead of funeral black, waved happily to the passing doughboys.

The Harlem regiment reached the banks of the Rhine on the morning of November 21. The troops were the first Allies to reach that famous river in western Germany. The fact that they could march unchallenged so far into the nation meant the war was really over.

Three weeks later, the 369th was back in France. There, the government awarded the regiment one of France's highest military honors, the Croix de Guerre. One hundred and seventy soldiers in the regiment also received individual medals for their bravery in battle.

AEF commanders resented the honors bestowed upon the African Americans and gave them the worst duties in the cleanup. Nine thousand black soldiers were assigned to the new military cemetery at Romagne. They searched the battlefield, picking up arms, legs,

Infantrymen receive medals for exceptional bravery. NATIONAL ARCHIVES

Soldiers bury the remains of Americans at the military cemetery in Romagne. NATIONAL ARCHIVES

and other body parts severed by exploding artillery shells. They also unearthed thousands of doughboys who had been hastily buried where they died. The corpses were reburied in twenty three-thousand new graves. Nearly half of all Americans killed in battle during World War I were buried at Romagne, France.

While waiting in Brest to board a transport for home, the Harlem regiment was harassed by military police, or MPs. The most serious incident occurred when a soldier from the 369th interrupted a military policeman's conversation to ask for directions. Angered by the black doughboy's forwardness, the MP hit the soldier with his billy club, fracturing his skull.

When Major Little complained to the MP, he was told that the "niggers were feeling their oats a bit . . . instructions had been given to take it out of them quickly, just as soon as they arrived, so as not to have trouble later on."

At the end of January, the 369th sailed for home. They arrived in New York on Lincoln's birthday, February 12, 1919. Five days later, the soldiers marched up Manhattan's famous Fifth Avenue.

Big Jim Europe's band, playing lively military tunes, led the parade. Behind the band came seventeen commissioned officers, including Colonel Hayward, limping from a war wound. They were followed by thirteen hundred black soldiers marching in French

Members of the 369th, happy to be on a ship going home NATIONAL ARCHIVES

The Hell Fighters parading up Manhattan's Fifth Avenue NATIONAL ARCHIVES

military formation. At the rear, riding in cars, were the men who had lost legs, been blinded, or suffered other severe wounds. Henry Johnson, wearing a shiny Croix de Guerre on his chest, rode in an open automobile and waved to the crowd.

Nearly a million people turned out along the seven-mile route from midtown Manhattan uptown to Harlem. "Looking at their faultless ranks stretching in perfect alignment from curb to curb, their dignified soldierly bearing," one newspaper reporter wrote, "it was hard to believe that less than two years ago many of these bemedaled veterans were parlor car porters, apartment house helpers, restaurant waiters, shipping clerks, bellboys, truck drivers, and what not."

The soldiers clearly loved being the center of attention. "That's one of the biggest men in New York," commented a doughboy parading past the Henry Clay Frick mansion at East Seventieth Street. "I used to shine his shoes. Now he's almost falling out of a window to wave to me."

The self-made regiment that began "without traditions, without education, and without friends," as its commander once remarked, had distinguished itself in the Great War. The 369th had been on the Western Front for 191 days, which was much longer than any other American unit. It never lost a foot of ground to the enemy, or had a man taken prisoner. But the distinguished record had come at a high price. Over half of the old Fifteenth New York had been killed or wounded.

Homecoming parades were held in many cities and towns across the United States, but the parade in Harlem was a little more special. The African Americans of the 369th had not only helped win the Great War, they had proven wrong the racists who had insisted black men would never be good combat troops.

Above 110th Street, where the Harlem community begins, the people cheered wildly for the parading soldiers. Harlem's population had doubled during the war years when plentiful jobs had caused a mass movement of black Southerners to northern cities. This movement was called the Great Migration. The crowd watching

The Great Migration

Hundreds of thousands of black Southerners moved to northern cities during World War I. This mass movement is called the Great Migration.

People left their poor southern homes for high paying jobs in the North. The European war had created a large demand for canned foods, steel, and manufactured goods. At the same time, the war had caused a shortage of labor in the slaughterhouses, steel mills, and factories.

The factory jobs had been taken by the millions of Irish, German, Polish, Russian, and Italian people who had immigrated to America in the decades between the Civil War and World War I. These immigrants filled the industrial cities in the Northeast and Midwest and provided the factories with plentiful, cheap labor. World War I cut off the flow of immigrants from Europe just as the need for factory laborers was increasing. Few factories had employed black workers, but that suddenly changed.

Migrants waiting for a northbound train crowd a "colored only" waiting room in a Florida station. FLORIDA STATE ARCHIVES

Southerners soon learned about the plentiful high paying jobs up north. The *Chicago Defender,* a widely read black-owned newspaper, published articles about the opportunities and pleasures enjoyed by Chicago's black community. And people who had already moved wrote letters home describing how much better their lives had become.

Most African Americans at the beginning of World War I lived in the southern United States. It was a segregated region where blacks lacked hospitals, schools, and police protection. They worked for low wages as field hands and maids, the same menial jobs their enslaved grandparents had performed. Although America's five million slaves had been freed during the Civil War a half century earlier, they had never become full–fledged citizens.

Southern blacks had long imagined the country above the Mason–Dixon Line to be a promised land where African Americans enjoyed greater freedom and equality. This belief and the new job opportunities encouraged blacks to migrate north.

The African American population on Chicago's South Side swelled from 50,000 to nearly 250,000. Detroit's black population quickly grew from a few thousand to over 100,000. New York's Harlem had been mostly white before 1910, but it was all black twenty years later.

Southern migrants learned that prejudice existed up north too, but they also found more opportunities. There were schools and jobs to help them build better lives. They could elect their own political representatives and openly protest against segregation and lynching.

World War I migrants created communities that attracted millions of black Southerners during the next half century. They knew the North was not a promised land, but it was a better land.

The 369th homecoming parade marches up Lenox Avenue in Harlem.
NATIONAL ARCHIVES

the parade in Harlem was estimated at a quarter of a million people. Children had been given the day off from school. Sidewalks, roofs, windows, and fire escapes overflowed with people.

When Jim Europe's band reached 130th Street, it stopped playing military music and began playing a popular jazz song, "Here Comes My Daddy." The crowd went wild with delight. "Mothers and wives and sisters and sweethearts recognized their boys and their men and they rushed right out through the ranks to join them," Major Little wrote in the final pages of his diary, "and we marched through Harlem singing and laughing."

Significant Events

1914   Archduke Franz Ferdinand assassinated June 28 in Sarajevo.
World War I begins July 28 when Austria declares war on Serbia.
Germany declares war on Russia August 1 and on France August 3.
President Woodrow Wilson says America will remain neutral.

1915   The Great Migration begins.
A U-boat sinks the *Lusitania,* May 7, killing 1,198 people.

1916   Woodrow Wilson, promising to keep America out of war, is elected to second term as president on November 7.

1917   The U.S. declares war on Germany April 6.
Selective Service enacted May 18.
National Guard mobilized July 3.

1918   Russia signs peace agreement with Germany March 3.
German army advances on Paris March 21.
The Ninety-second and Ninety-third Divisions land in France over a five-month period.
The battle of the Meuse-Argonne begins September 26.
Armistice signed at 11 A.M. November 11.

1919   Two million American doughboys return home.

Further Reading

Barbeau, Arthur E. *The Unknown Soldiers: African American Troops in World War I* (New York: Da Capo Press, 1996).

Bosco, Peter. *World War I* (New York: Facts on File, 1991).

Clare, John D. ed. *First World War* (New York: Harcourt Brace, 1994).

Friedel, Frank. *Over There: The Story of America's First Great Overseas Crusade* (Philadelphia: Temple University Press, 1990).

Gay, Kathlyn, and Martin Gay. *World War I* (New York: Twenty-First Century Books, 1995).

Little, Arthur W. *From Harlem to the Rhine: The Story of New York's Colored Volunteers* (New York: Haskell House Publishers Ltd., 1974).

Index

Page numbers in *italics* refer to map and photos.

69